This book belongs to:

Kennedy

A humane can do enething

Inat ones was a turkey
who was vary skard
of jil Anumys it was
but the kidshing
he got hes legs soa humf
help him he got fuc tod

A humane can doe verthing

Barn it was skare but
the humane und ~~do~~
sumthing so it did do sumthin
it caryit to the humane
debrom it was so kool
it had a ranjoe silr and alotmor

Don't let the

Made in the USA
Coppell, TX
10 August 2021